a participant° guide
MEDIA

INSIDE THE NEW YORK TIMES

PAGE ONE

AND THE FUTURE OF JOURNALISM

EDITED BY

DAVID FOLKENFLIK

PUBLICAFFAIRS
New York

Published in the United States by PublicAffairs™, a Member of the Perseus Books Group
All rights reserved.
Printed in the United States of America.

PublicAffairs books are available at special discounts for bulk purchases in the U.S. by corporations, institutions, and other organizations. For more information, please contact the Special Markets Department at the Perseus Books Group, 2300 Chestnut Street, Suite 200, Philadelphia, PA 19103, call (800) 810-4145, ext. 5000, or e-mail special.markets@perseusbooks.com.

The Library of Congress has cataloged the printed edition as follows:
ISBN 978-1-58648-960-1 (PB)
ISBN 978-1-61039-077-4 (EB)

Library of Congress Control Number: 2011928719

First Edition

10 9 8 7 6 5 4 3 2 1